A Shark at the Pool

by Sascha Goddard

illustrated by Gareth Conway

OXFORD
UNIVERSITY PRESS
AUSTRALIA & NEW ZEALAND

It was a hot morning. Nan took Max to the pool.

Look at me, Nan!

Max met Ben at the pool.

Max took Nan to the deep part of the pool.

Look at me shoot up!

Nan had a turn. She shot up, too.

Nan took off. She was quick.

Nan shot up in the hoop.

Max shot up to hurl the fish.

zoom

13

Then Max got a shock.

Is it a fin?

A shark in the pool!